Journey Of The Mind, Heart, And Soul

Poems of Faith, Youth, and Heartbreak

Edarly Elizabeth Edouard

/ BookLeaf
Publishing

India | USA | UK

Made with ❤ on the BookLeaf Publishing Platform
www.bookleafpub.in
www.bookleafpub.com

Dedication

To every reader who resonates with the words spoken in every page, may you find the joy of reading and relating to every word I write.

Preface

Every page is a story of my life, and I hope all who read it will relate to the words conveyed in every page. Every raw emotion and prayers of the soul will be conveyed in this book. I hope you like what you read and relate to it somehow.

Acknowledgements

The gift of writing is a treasure for me when words are in vain. Thank you to BookLeaf Publishing for letting me have the opportunity to convey every emotion I feel into one book.

1. Music, A Soothing Sound

Nothing is more soothing than the echoes of music,
It delivers more than just notes on a sheet,
The pacifying sounds are purer than the sea waves,
It's the humble portrayal of love and peace.
I ponder underneath the sapphire skies,
Reposing on a vivid bed of blooms
Then I register my psyche to its fine melodies
To attend to my famished gloom.

I am consoled by the mystical cuddles of my Zephyr
As it peacefully croons a seraph tune,
It is my ethereal choir: the graceful echo of a crescendo,
The decency through all conflict keeps me immune.
It is my sweet supreme satisfaction,
Tis the essence of clarity.
The ultimate power of healing and restoration,
The recuperation of a broken memory.

Its radiance renders me reassurance,
Tuning out the disgraceful environment,

My tune is my island of romanticism
Denying the songs of anguish.
It is the manifestation of composure,
Renovating my lonesome soul,
Life changing and heartening,
And sweeter than the honeycomb.

My harmony is my reassuring sanctuary,
No battle can harm me there.
Despondency and war may have its ways,
But I am defended by its breastplates of care.
I treasure the purest voices of all voices,
For its legacy is boundless,
After all has passed, it remains a soothing sound,
Enchanting and curing all that is broken.

2. Youth

Your youth is never a solid promise;
even friendships are seldom permanent.
You hail me as if I am a goddess,
deeming that my loveliness is certain.

The way you narrate me with sympathy
has no force o'er the frenzied years ahead.
Like petals stripped from its anatomy,
my youth will recede until I am dead.

To you, I am effortless to describe
when I am young like the skyline's daybreak.
If my youth can no longer be revived,
do you compare me to a summer's day?

I cannot control the folds on my brows,
But my splendor is as sure as my vows.

3. No One Notices

She daydreams throughout the daylight,
And has wishes of feeling precious and valued;
She needs the universe to comprehend her emotions,
She is desperate for someone to stroke her delicately and
benevolently whisper:
"Why do you seem so discouraged, my dear?"

She's as tranquil as the seawaters and as tender as the
doves,
She is but a keen-eyed youngster pursuing affection,
She feels secluded and forlorn; all she seeks is soothing
consolation,
But the world's in utter obliviousness;
Not one being lingers for the likes of her.

She is struggling how to associate securely with other
mortals,
Her fears are conquering a vast portion of her character,
She needs someone to recognize her internal soreness,
But she is nothing short of a quiet creature.

Is silence really golden?

Nothing appears to be terminating her despondency,
She looks around the vivid atmosphere,
Hoping to see if there is anyone who'll provide her
reassurance,
But no one stops for her; she feels despised,
So she lies beneath the beaming sun on a massive fertile
bed of grassland,
Only to shed tears.

She buries her face in her arms, but no one notices,
She plants a fake smile on her face, but no one notices.
The world fails to consult her of her uncertainties and
traps,
Feebly, she reaches for courage to find her,
She never ceases seeking for friendship and bliss.
Hope is what she relentlessly longs for.
This is all that her grieving heart desires.

Still, no one notices.

She strays through the jade scenery,
Listening to the birds above serenading their birdsongs
of ecstasy,
While she strays lonely as a powdery mist in the sky.

She weeps a puddle of gloomy streams,
As she is in solitude, preserving a broken heart.
She bawls in perpetual despair,
Hoping someone out there might deliver cheerfulness
To her melancholic heart.

Even so, no one notices.

4. Comforting

Concerned was the stranger as she noticed tears
streaming down my eyes,
One day, I came home drenched in utter despondency
and labor,
My heart was desperate for some type of relaxation, but
all I could
Find was, on my table, a black pen and a white sheet of
paper.
Overwhelmed with compassion, the stranger asked me
for my name,
Reluctant was I, for I was skeptical about what she could
possibly do,
Time to time, she insisted, until I finally picked up my
writing utensil,
It was then I had learned to let my feelings out; relief
was then coming through.
Never had I realized that she was willing to offer me an
unusual kind of peace,
Grateful and relieved, I asked her for her name, and she
told me "Poetry."

5. Love Again

We've heard the overstressed promises,
"I'm here for you"
and "You won't go through this alone,"
at some point in our lives.
These are, what I call,
the interchangeable themes of
hope and togetherness.
Love has taught us that
our burdens should be shared and understood,
Cared for and cultivated,
but what is "understanding" without "STANDING,"
And "trust" without "US?"
Why have we been so oblivious
to the cries for help from those who need it?
Must you fulfill your own desires,
and put the disadvantaged on your waiting list?
What kind of inconsiderate individual
would have the decency
to say to his brother
without shame, without regret,

"I have no blood for you, brother?"
Hatred makes its home within
those whose cup is overflowed
with shame and sin.
If love does not dishonor others,
why can't we make it the center of our hearts,
if one is willing to accept it,
if one is willing to live for it,
if one is willing to DIE for it,
if they know what love *really* is?
We must not let the infernos
of bitterness
extinguish the love we must have
for our neighbors, and for ourselves.
No matter what our origins are,
it doesn't change the fact that
we are all one,
we are all human,
we are all blessed,
and we are all loved.
When will we comprehend the idea
that black and white are just words
that we allow ourselves to believe
when we see each other in the flesh?
When will we learn the truth
that we are all just
different shades of brown?

When will we learn,
at the end of the day,
that we all cut and bleed the same color "red?"
When will we learn to surrender
our pessimistic thoughts
to our Creator,
in this hand-width scuffle we call "life?"
Why must we turn our backs on
the force that led our Father to die on a cross
with His arms wide open
for those whom He loves?
We must set an example
for those who were born after us,
so that they themselves can teach their children
the wisdom and judgment
needed in this troubled atmosphere.
Teach them that
no worldwide festivity
that comes once a year
should be a sign for them
to perform good will,
for love is an uninterrupted mission
that we all must fulfill.
Teach them that love is not a set of rules,
or a stack of notes you jot down in a notebook.
It is a way of life,
a way of reminding each other that,

no, we are not perfect,
but we empathize with you,
and we genuinely care.
What we stand for
and what we believe in
is our decision,
but it should not stand
between the love that we must have
for one another,
as sisters and brothers.
I give this message of hope
to those who haven't quite yet understood
the beauty in diversity.
We can love again,
this time, not just with words,
but with our actions.
This is truly how
we can have justice for the fallen,
compassion for the destitute,
and comfort for the brokenhearted.
If we can do this,
love wouldn't be a religion,
but a sincere, devoted relationship,
and a rock-solid THREAT
to the influencers of revulsion.
Make time for friendship and harmony,
and the schemes of the Other Side

will shatter to the floor
like broken glass that fails
to revive itself.
Let's make our love for each other
vivid like the Sun,
but brighter than its beauty,
and stronger than its formidable beams.
If we can all commit to this,
we can be a generation
that finally learns to love,
with a love that should already be ours.

6. No being on earth can liken to you

No being on earth can liken to you,
Your presence makes even blossoms rejoice.
The rarity of your zest I pursue,
Like the tenor of your entrancing voice.

Like a sailor lost in the mighty dusk,
Adrift am I beholding your keen eyes.
You lifted me out of the gritty dust,
As a kite being launched into the sky.

Though doom may separate us like the walls,
Our union becomes stronger day by day.
Though we may shudder, we refuse to fall
Like a lighthouse during a hurricane.

Your presence remedied my lonesomeness,
May my healing psyche laud your boldness.

7. Belittling

Frequently, you were told that
you don't have what it takes to be enough.
Those with little hearts
belittle you so much until it cuts deep
like a wound that never heals.
They criticize your anatomy,
telling you constantly
that you must be such to mean much.
They twist their words around
to make the wrong sound right,
and the right wrong.
When it finally gets to you,
you find yourself at home
sobbing in your pillow
until the salty tear stains are as massive
as the hole in your heart.
You then start allowing
yourself to believe what you're not.
"No one cares about me.
I am worthless, like an ancient

piece of jewelry left to rust."
You finally decide to stop crying
when your eyes weighed more
than your broken heart.
You had to make that decision
yourself
since no one was around
to reassure you,
whether they knew about
your grief or not.
Your entire life
Was a game
With no players.
Your mistakes were a lesson
With no support.
Your tears were an expression
With no comfort.

8. Final Hour

No life on earth shall be threatened by greed
When the value of every second counts.
If the promise of life was guaranteed,
Why have we surrendered to crime and doubt?

The land that exists for all humankind
was not built on the grounds of prejudice.
Like a gloomy shadow when the sun shines,
Sin takes a stride with those who allow it.

Reprimanding a human by the neck
Is leaving a helpless toddler to drown.
Why must we be unfair to each other
When we are all just diverse shades of brown?

Why fight for what should already be ours?
Let's grow in love in this final hour.

9. The Fragile Dance of Triumph

"Now she can hardly walk. How long do you think it will
be till the slumber comes?"
Not a single being can tell, for many have attempted to
race the clock,
But passed before their time even arrived.

As for Princess Meryl,
the effects of her achievements could not be suppressed.
Her hair is powdery like the snowy-white mountains in
Australia,
And tis the prize of triumph.
Her eyes are as gray as the beamy illumination of the
moon,
but all she pays attention to is the magnificence of life.
Her face is not as youthful as it used to be,
but her skin glows as stunning as the stars in the
midnight blue atmosphere.
On the outside, she is fragile and frail,
but on the inside, she is spontaneous and satisfied.

Mankind pictures her as an overdue mortal,
but to the ones she's intimate with, she is an example of
a life well-lived.

Never has she questioned "Why," for her faith
overshadowed her doubts,
much like how the waterways of love extinguish the
infernos of hate.
Never has she ever permitted the infernos of vengeance
to dominate her soul,
for she's made peace with the reality that she conquered
what her adversaries couldn't.
Every now and then, tears flood down her face like drops
of rain coursing down a window,
because her bravery throughout the years brought her
gratitude and joy.

Don't worry about the accommodations of life; learn to
make memories out of them."
"Learning from the best," she says, "is the greatest lesson
of life."
From that moment, I knew she fulfilled her greatest
destiny.
Though she could hardly walk, it is her fearlessness that
walked with her.

10. Can I go back to when I was young?

Can I go back to when I was young?
I miss all the times I played under the sun.
I remember the days of board games and P.E.,
And the memories of friends—all so bittersweet.
Who can forget all the childhood tv shows,
Watching them all from the comfort of home?
Relaxing and lying comfortably in bed,
Tucked in like the bonnet around my head.
Oh how I miss the days that were, in every way, better,
Oh how I miss the days when my parents were together.
Santa, Disney, Holy Land—all the best of days,
All the moments before Grandpa passed away.
Oh how I miss his humor and the thrill of his presence,
Like the faces of friends I haven't seen in a moment.
Now I'm living like a robot working every single day,
All the while tricking my mind into thinking I'm okay.
So many responsibilities to bear while feeling broken,
My brain feels like a browser with too many tabs open.
I missed the days when all I could think about was

goofing off,
Now I'm faced with the reality that the god ole days are
gone.
Now I don't even have time to freely breathe in the
soothing air
And feel the calming breeze flowing through my curly
hair.
Now my hair is falling out like sand slipping through my
fingers
From all the pressure and hopelessness that seems to
really linger.
Take me back to when I lived in my imagination,
Unbound from the stress of all the chaos and trepidation.

11. Soothing Tensions: A Dance of Sound

A contemporary, yet influential mechanism brought to
Earth,
its anatomy remains unchanged,
generation after generation.
Press, and at your command,
a melodious tune commences.
Hold, and the sound lingers
until it disintegrates like a haze of an invisible breeze.
Its tune's radiance renders me reassurance,
As it releases the graceful echo of a crescendo.
Play one triad after another in a disciplined manner,
And you hear a pacifying sound
that is purer than the sea waves on the horizon.
The more pressure applied to each sound,
The more dynamic is the outcome.
Bizarre when all is played at once,
yet soothing when in sync.
Tis the tone of tranquility at the expense of tension.

12. The Fading of My Woodland Crown

I took pleasure in my crown of glory,
The resilience of my roots,
The liveliness of my strands.
I once walked through my woodland
Admiring every individual strand
Looking like a crown of springs.
Every curl towered over each other,
An explosion of curls as the wind flirted with it.
Every sapling grew so close together
That no land was visible.
But alas, my coronet of splendor fades,
And day by day, strands are falling out.
My scalp was filled with springy curls,
But now notice the denseness of my forest.
Bit by bit, my trees are stripped
And curly strands are left on my pillow
Like a bird's broken nest.
I tried new shampoos, oils,
and other broken promises,

But the same disheartening view
My eyes behold each morning.
Something that belonged to me,
I now must let go.
It's more than vanity,
although that stings.
But no lost strand
Is worth the Beholder's beloved.
I whisper to the fear,
"The sky is still blue,
And beauty lives beyond
My fading crown.
Take heart, for my forest
Will return to its former glory,
But not without acceptance
Of the fight to restoration."

13. Nature's Symphony

The daylight turns to dull darkness,
The clouds increase in bulk and thicken up like smoke.
An earthly aroma penetrates my nostrils,
The scent of the earth exhaling.
The smell of life and minerals
Reveal a brewing storm.
Eavesdrop to the booming drummers upstairs,
Commanding authority and fear in every rumble.
See the angry bright veins
illuminating the gloomy atmosphere,
Setting off an astronomical shred in the sky.
Gaze at the blubbers of the blues,
the sounds of water bombs striking the ground.
Watch land appearing soggy like a carpet of muck
And the streets becoming shimmering canals.
The pavement became as smooth as a layer of glass,
With water running down it in rivulets.
The force of nature manifests itself as an engulfing gale,
Obstructing the display of a wonderful world,
Turning a luminous landscape into a wall of water

outside my window.
The transformation of the firmament was quite a sight to
see;
The rainclouds were saturated like a ballon ready to
burst.
Then my view was much clearer,
As I noticed a silver of blue peeking through
Like a timid eye, watching the earth awaken.
And I saw a wave of vivid colors painted across the sky,
as the sulky pillows above gently disintegrated.
The view was as mighty as the Great Artist Himself,
As His promises of hope and comfort came to be.
Puddles reflected the sky,
Resembling a broken mirror on the soaking surface.
Raindrops are clinging
Like jewels on the tree branches.
The rain show came to a halt,
And I once again saw the Sun,
Hear the birds sing a little louder.
The air smelled fresh and new
Like the first breath of spring.
And there was nothing but a picturesque scenery,
The best my eyes have ever gazed upon.

14. Lessons in the Shadows of Shame

My past was filled with anger
that I had a hard time letting go,
but it was also filled with friends
who taught me how to grow.
I used to roam so many places
like an eagle unafraid of heights,
and now, I'm sitting on my bed
thinking what's wrong with my life.
Life was waiting for me to answer,
Yet all along, I was insecure.
Now that things are passing me by,
I realized I could've been so much more.
All the friends I've had back then
A helping hand I've held too tight
The gentle kindness that I once knew
Has now faded into the night.
I kept way too many promises
that I knew I would break later.
I used to think of myself as hard-working,

but I'm nothing more than a procrastinator.
I should've listened to the signs
when they were first given to me,
but now, I look at myself in shame,
thinking, "This could've been your dream."
I blame myself for everything
because I didn't try hard enough.
Who knew that repeating third grade
would cost you so much?
The pressure built inside of me
is becoming agonizing like an itchy wound,
but I must keep reminding myself
that it will all be better soon.
My mind is filled with doubts,
and all the things I prayed against.
Even though I am hurting inside,
I'm confident that it's not the end.
One little setback in life
can make you question your purpose,
but if you hold on tight to that end of the string,
then no obstacle can undermine your courage.
It's difficult trying to stay positive
in a world filled with despair and stress,
but every time I cry, I remind myself that
my heart is still beating inside of my chest.

15. Stubborn Stains of Authority

"Time is not your friend, and neither am I,"
mumbles our boss as she walks around us.
The sound of her footsteps
is like a drumbeat
On the floorboards.
Her eyes are as cold as the temperature in the room
That she refuses to adjust.
The fear of her presence
builds up inside of me
like the faucet in our break room;
slow at first, then a steady, relentless stream.
We shrink in our chairs,
Not one of us daring to make eye contact.
We pray for five o'clock,
But it's eight in the morning.
Meetings look more like interrogations
Than an innocent partnership.
Ideas are shredded before they bloom,
Like a house of sand,

Crumbling into useless bits.
A mountain of tasks assigned to us,
Expectations higher than our nerves around her.
Her arrogance was like an endless, droning lecture
By a know-it-all.
Her makeup and good looks
Don't cover the foulness of her heart.
Why is she like this?
Reprimanding me over every little mistake I do,
As if she hasn't made them all herself.
Nothing will ever be enough for her.
She's as stubborn as the stains on her heart.

16. Gone

A group of friends,
The time we've spent
Together,
The fun things we did
Being together
Like a song
Where the harmonies blend
And voices soar.
We were the eyes
That saw the same world
Together.
The pictures, the music,
The food we ate
Together.
The board games,
The prayer sessions,
Holding hands
Together.
All poignant, all memorable,
All fragile, all gone.

Our loved one
We spent time with,
The bond we shared
Together.
Grandpa's rocking chair,
Silent in the living room.
The scent of his cologne
Faded now.
His favorite hat,
Hanging in the closet,
Gathering dust,
A memory's cloak.
The ticking of the grandfather clock
Grows more faint
Like the sound of his voice.
All the memories
Captured my psyche
Like a story I can't put down.
All poignant, all memorable.
All fragile, all gone.

The notebook
Given to me
By my dearest friend,
So touching, so thoughtful
Like the warm blanket

She gave me
That Sunday morning.
What a friendship,
Held on tight,
But way too tight.
Alas, my grip is gone.

Precious moments,
Hold them close,
Like the ones beside you,
Before the night is gone.

17. Dreams

I took a picture of my dreams
Dark in the night
With my canvas open,
Fatigued yet inspired,
Frail yet motivated.
With my utensil in hand
And a lens to capture,
Stories be told.
Point and click and write,
With a memory to chase
In the dark.
The screen shows only
My bedroom wall,
Dull paint imitating the nocturnal gloom,
And the moonlight through my window,
As bright as a diamond flame.
Yet this seed in my chest
Has yet to bloom,
Something remains
That my canvas beholds.

Maybe the picture wasn't taken,
But planted,
Deep in my heart,
For it to grow.
Dreams fade like smoke,
And through my window
A morning light appears.
It awakens me,
The picture is gone,
But when sleep returns,
May I find it again,
And paint my picture
Crystal clear.

18. Forbidden Siesta

I see the moon stuck in the sky,
A silver coin in the atmosphere.
It illuminates my room
Like a bleached powdery blaze.
I'm on my bed
With sheets tangled,
I'm a restless ocean wave.
The planet's in deep slumber,
But I'm awake, three hours
Past the world's curfew.
I hear my A.C. running,
The house is breathing deep
Like a slumbering giant,
While my eyes are still open.
Dead silence across the room
Interrupted by
My pondering and rustling.
My mind's become a screen,
It flickers and glows,
With memories and regrets.

It doesn't seem to end,
The songs of agitation
Playing through my mind,
A sarcastic cradlesong.
Another hour passes by,
As I await the blaze of
The morning sun,
Yet it feels like forever.
When will this sleep claim its own?
The clock is ticking
Like a steady drum,
When will this forbidden siesta
Become unforbidden?
Perhaps a dream will find its way
To my chaotic mind.
May the calmness of
The gloomy night
Grant my soul the slumber it needs.

19. A Beacon in the Gloom

The hole in my heart, so heavy, so vast,
Was this lonely trail meant to last?
This heavy shroud I drag around
And haunts me 'til I hit the ground.
But then I see a brilliant light
Shining like a beacon, hopeful tonight.
A hesitant step, one after the other,
A guiding light lifting me out of the gutter.
With a voice quivering like a leaf,
I struggle to release a frantic plea,
"Can anyone hear this voice torn apart?
Who can break this fortress around my heart?"
Then a friendly face with a helping hand,
Tells me in love, "I understand,"
Embraces me with friendship's flowers
When I thought I saw my final hour.
The walls may collapse stone by stone,
But in their place, a greenhouse is grown.
Yes it's scary to let others in
To show the scars from deep within.

Yet opening up is not a fall,
But breaking chains, releasing all.
Let this be an open space
To talk it out, face to face.

20. Perpetual Suffering

The day was brief, and quick time flies,
Thunder booming, rain bucketing from the skies,
The stony classroom was set to thirty degrees
We've spent five tedious hours with nothing to eat

Mr. Spring is as sturdy as sticks and stones
Bulldozing us until we break our bones
Conceited was he, assigning work pile by pile
Terrorizing us with labor that's not even worth our
while

Surrounded by closed windows and blue wallpapers
As cobalt as the ocean and watery like vapor
The covers on the wall feel like a hollow utopia
The water drops behind it embolden a sloping
melancholia

"Focus wisely," roared Mr. Spring, "The stakes are too
high,
Focus on the questions right before your very eyes"

The man of impulse grumbles in a deep hearty voice,
"Review all of your answers, if you rely on the right
choice"

A thick book trying to grasp our attention
Strained to undergo a thousand pages of apprehension
Glaring at an exam when we should be in the open air
Each question asked puts my peace to fatal despair

So many hours with nothing to eat,
Why does learning feel more like defeat?
He marks our papers, red with hate,
Sealing our academic fate.

Insignificant to a professor, solitary in the real world
Trained to become a woman, no longer just a girl
All things considered, I found my biggest rivalry:
The complex nature of perpetual suffering.

21. What Once Was, And What Shall Come

I'm utterly ashamed of our land,
I thought we would prevail over the odds.
We were once a hospitable homeland where we
welcomed all humankind the opportunity to call this
nation their home,
We built our castles then of sand, believing the tide
would never rise.
But now the castles have crumbled, and we've become
our own worst enemies, denying foreigners the access to
a better life in this so-called "free world."
I remember the golden times when we would all come
together in every situation, lifting each other's spirits by
telling one another that no matter how frenzied and
hectic the years ahead will be, everything would be
okay...eventually.
I remembered when people would selflessly help others,
even if it meant risking time for themselves.
I remember the songs we had sung together and the joy
it would bring,

But now it seems to exist only in my dreams.
Every memory of togetherness stings like a bee as I see
my neighbors belittled like a broken toy.
Why have we lost the decency and the morality to care
for those who can't care for themselves?
Why have we been too busy showing off when we all
could have spent our time showing love?
The selfless heart of a giver should be enough to
eradicate the evils caused by the selfish heart of a greedy
person.
The impermanence of life should remind us all that all
our commotion over one thing after another ends in
nothing, like meadows reduced to ashes.
Yet I am optimistic that the flag still waves red, white,
and blue, so let the promise of justice and hope prevail.
I am aware that hope is a fragile bird, and the streets are
divided, but let's answer liberty's call together, once and
for all.